THE $HARP ENTREPRENEUR

LUCY WARIARA

First Published in July 2021

ISBN: 978-93-5427-586-9

BLUEROSE PUBLISHERS

www.bluerosepublishers.com

info@bluerosepublishers.com

+91 8882 898 898

Cover Design:

Lucy Wariara

Typographic Design:

Namrata Saini

Distributed by: BlueRose, Amazon, Flipkart, Shopclues

This book is dedicated to my sons Michael Chai and David Chai for teaching me the true meaning of unconditional love.

Acknowledgments

This book wouldn't have been possible without the support and encouragement of people who believed in me.

I thank David Chai for contributing on one of the chapters, and providing detailed and constructive comments in all the chapters.

I thank Wangari Kiluva and Hannah Gitonga-Mwangi for taking time to review and discuss the text, as well as clarifying concepts and explaining the rationale for specific recommendations.

I thank my role model Robert Kiyosaki, businessman and author whose teachings on entrepreneurship inspired me to not only be an entrepreneur, but to also be a teacher.

I thank friends and relatives who encouraged me. I heard it all and it meant a lot to me.

I thank Catherine Njeri for creating the symbol of 'Life is for the living' the series under which this book falls under.

I thank Bluerose Publishers for the valuable expertise provided in publishing of the book.

Finally, I thank my sons for keeping my dream of authoring this book alive, and making the journey and destination worthwhile.

Preface

I love to travel, and one thing I appreciate most whenever I visit a new country, is the work of people who use their talent to earn a living by creating pieces of music, paintings, sculptures, clothes, cakes, decoration pieces; you name it, the list goes on and on. In some of these places, it is evident that these people live a comfortable life from their earnings, but in other places, including where I live, there is a sense of them struggling to make ends meet, yet their products are equally good, if not better.

This got me wondering and asking why the discrepancy exists. After speaking to a few people, I learned that the difference between these two categories of people is that one has an entrepreneurial mindset while the other does not.

During a visit to Italy, I bought two beautiful silver rings from a tiny gift shop situated along a narrow alley in Venice. Mia, the owner of the shop was a young lady who had studied accounts in college, but her passion was in making jewellery and accessories. At the time of meeting her, she had been in business for three years. I learned that most of her clients were tourists, and she supplied her products at an exclusive fashion shop in Florence city.

Mia is a creative entrepreneur who sells necklaces, earrings, rings, pendants, and anklets made from silver and other materials. From interacting with her and observing how she conducted her business; I knew right away that the success of her business was pegged on her being able to work with creativity and think like an entrepreneur.

I offer this book as a resource on how to develop an entrepreneurial mindset so that you can manage and fully utilize your talent and skills in a more profitable way. After reading the book, you will be able to think about what you are doing and why, where you would like your business to lead you, and know exactly what you need to do to succeed.

An entrepreneurial mindset is the engine that generates creativity and innovation to the level where you are able to use your talent to earn money, and live a comfortable life.

This book is for…

- ***People who want to turn their hobby into a business.*** You will learn how to tap into your talent in innovative and creative ways, so that you can start earning money from your hobby.
- ***Freelancers who want to increase the number of clients.*** You will learn how to package what you have to offer, so you can reach more people and increase your income as a freelancer.
- ***Solopreneurs who want to grow their businesses.*** You will learn how to add value to your products, so you can form strategic partnerships that will allow you to diversify your products and grow your business.
- ***Anyone who has been thinking of starting a business.*** You will see business opportunities where others may not, and this will inspire you to start a business.

Regardless of where you fit in, I invite you to discover the benefits of having an entrepreneurial mindset, to help place you in a better position to use your talent and skills in a profitable way.

Contents

Introduction

Welcome to a new reality of doing business

As much as talent counts, effort counts twice.*— Angela Duckworth, academic, psychologist and author*

Imagine for a moment, a reality of doing business where:

- You could use your talent to make money
- You have access to the right information that will help you to succeed as an entrepreneur
- You know how to strike a balance between executing the technical part of your work, and managing the entrepreneurial aspect of your business
- You have the right resources that enable you to reach and engage with your customers
- You are able to meet the increasing demand for your products

This book is for people who want to use their talents to make money. The information is packaged in a way that allows readers to gain an understanding of how to develop an entrepreneurial mindset.

The book demonstrates how you can use your talent to make money, with the understanding that people operating within the creatives industry need to know how to be sharp entrepreneurs. A sharp entrepreneur is someone who is able to work with a lot of creativity, and think like a business person at the same time.

The first part of the book focuses on the creative side of doing business and provides an insight into various business opportunities within the creatives industry. This is followed by self-leadership skills that a sharp entrepreneur should have, to be able to successfully run a business.

The second part of the book looks at the money-making side of doing business, using innovation and improvement approaches, to keep the business running. It also provides information on how to get people to know and buy your products, as well as how to set up a basic bookkeeping system for your business.

The third part of the book contains Worksheets that will help you put what you have learned into perspective. The worksheets have leading questions and tasks for your input to guide you in setting up your business. Worksheet one will guide you on how to develop an entrepreneurial mindset. Worksheet two will guide you on how to assess available opportunities within the market, and to plan how your business will make money.

Many people operating within the creatives industry have the potential of becoming successful entrepreneurs, but they do not know where to start, and this hinders them from living up to their full potential. If this has been your perspective, this book will help you to develop an entrepreneurial mindset, a key component for becoming a sharp entrepreneur.

So, if you are someone who uses or is aspiring to start using your talent and passion to make money, read on to begin the journey of becoming a sharp entrepreneur within the creatives industry.

PART ONE

THE CREATIVE SIDE OF DOING BUSINESS

1

Creatives Industry Entrepreneurs

Creating the next level of results requires the next level of thinking.*— Rory Vaden, New York Times bestselling author*

Imagine living in a world without art, music, fashion, and crafts. How boring would life be! When we look at each separately, we see that art is everywhere, and it makes the places we live in and visit more colourful and interesting. Music is a universal language, that when we listen to, arouses different emotions that uplift our spirit and fills the heart with joy. Fashion is the language of human expression. What we wear says a lot about who we are or who we aspire to be. Crafts is the language of handmade materials that makes us appreciate the beauty and the value of things.

Art, music, fashion, and crafts are created by people who are talented in what they do. Their creation plays a big role in our society by providing us with solutions, entertainment, and pleasure.

People operating within the creatives industry are not only creative; they have a lot of potential for being successful entrepreneurs. They can use their creativity to build businesses that are fully centred around creativity.

Creative entrepreneurs can use their talents to make money. But they first need to have a good understanding of the industry, to be able to set up businesses and function as entrepreneurs.

Like in any other industry, the creatives industry has many opportunities for entrepreneurs to set up and run businesses.

Entrepreneurs in the Creatives Industry

Most entrepreneurs operating within the creatives industry are self-employed and run businesses in music, fashion, visual arts, photography, writing, film, etc. They produce products that people are willing to pay for.

I met Leon when he joined my former place of work as an intern in the communications department. During his free time, he used to paint abstract art that he sold to his customers. Over the weekends, Leon used to exhibit his work at art galleries, and within a short time, orders started streaming in from hotels and restaurants. By the time his internship was coming to an end after three months, he could barely keep up with work in the office, because orders for his paintings were many.

Years later, I bumped into Leon at a restaurant, and he told me that he never looked for a job after his internship, because he decided to run his painting business full time.

Leon is an example of an entrepreneur who has built a business around his talent. Creative entrepreneurs who are able to use their talent in a similar way are able to:

- Get paid to do something they love
- Have control over how and when they want to work
- Build a career that fits within their lifestyle goals

Now that we know who a creatives entrepreneur is, we need to know how they make money. To do this, we will explore opportunities within three divisions that are aligned to the creatives industry. These are music, fashion, and visual arts.

Music Industry

Without music, there would be no industry to build on, which means that there would be no room for entrepreneurship.

Individuals and corporations around the world have built fortunes on the understanding of how the music industry operates. In this section, we will look at various entrepreneurial opportunities within the music industry, how they complement each other, and how you can find your preference if you want to pursue a career in music.

Individuals and corporations have built fortunes on the understanding of how the music industry operates.

The music industry is made up of various fields such as recording artists, producers, recording engineers, songwriters, and composers. It is worth noting that an individual can operate in all these fields, although this is not commonly done. This is because each field is highly specialized and requires a lot of investment in terms of resources and time.

Recording Artist

A recording artist is someone who records vocals on a piece of music. This is the person who is seen as the face of the music when promoting the finished product. An example of a well-known recording artist is Drake, a Canadian-born artist who has recorded multiple award-winning Pop and Hip-hop, and RnB albums. Although his major contribution in most of these albums is his vocals, he also deserves credit for writing most of his songs.

Producer

Music production is made up of three categories, and each has a producer. The executive producer oversees the financing of the song, while the vocal producer oversees the vocal aspects of the song. The music producer, also known as a record producer, is responsible for managing the recording and production of the music for a single artist or a band.

The role of the music producer ranges from producing one song to an entire album, with the producer focusing on sound recording, pre-production, and mixing the audio of the song.

Recording Engineer

A recording engineer, also known as an audio engineer is a technical specialist who sets up and operates the equipment that records, mixes, edits, and reproduces sound. This is the technical guru responsible for ensuring that the sound quality of the music is of a high standard.

Songwriter

A songwriter is an individual who writes the lyrics of a song that is recorded by a recording artist. Many recording artists write their lyrics, but there are also just as many artists who lack the expertise of composing their lyrics to a given song. This is where the role of a songwriter comes in handy.

Composer

This is an individual who is an author of music in any form, including vocal or instrumental music, creating in any of the given genres and often presenting his music in a written musical score using music notation.

Composers are also skilled performers of music. It is worth noting that this is a dying form of music production since the digital era has more or less made the composer's role obsolete. This is because music has become more digitally produced, taking the place of art forms such as music notation, which is the reading and writing of music in a musical stave.

Business Side of Music

As previously indicated, an individual can master various fields within the music industry, but this is not a simple task. It is therefore important to find what suits you and begin your career of creating musical art.

Since we have covered the production side of music, we will now focus on the business side of music. In this section, we look at different occupations that exist within the music business. These are in addition to what we have already covered in music production for recording artists, producers, recording engineers, songwriters, and composers. We will also look at how you can make money from your music.

Setting the record straight

The biggest myth in the music industry is that knowing how to make music means that you understand the music business. This is not true. In fact, the inverse serves to be more of the truth. Most musicians do not understand how the music business works, that is how to market and sell their products to the larger masses. This creates room for entrepreneurs who understand how to make a living from music that has been produced by someone else—to operate within the music industry.

Another myth is that the only source of income in the music industry is the songs made by the artists. In today's world, the total sum of money made from a recorded song accounts for the smallest amount of income earned by an artist and the team.

The truth of the matter is, there are many ways of making money within the music business ranging from an independent artist, artist manager, music lawyer, and record label, among others.

Independent recording artist

An independent recording artist is also known as an unsigned recording artist. This is a recording artist who has chosen not to sign up with any record label and personally manages the distribution of his music. Doing this can serve to be beneficial or detrimental to the recording artists, depending on how much effort is put into the entrepreneurship of their products.

Most musicians start as unsigned recording artists. If you have a catalogue of music ranging to hundreds, yet you have not signed a contract that puts you under a record label, it means that you are operating as an independent recording artist. The question is, how then can you make money as an independent recording artist?

There are many ways for recording artists to make money from their music, and earning royalties is one of them, made up of four types of royalties. These are mechanical, public performance, synchronization, and print music. The music industry relies on these royalties as the main source of income for musicians.

As a recording artist, you can maintain the royalties of all your songs and earn from them over the years. Many artists still earn from the music they produced many years ago.

Streaming music on digital music platforms such as Spotify and YouTube is another way for recording artists to make money from the number of streams their music tracks have. A stream is a name given to a single play of a song within a given streaming service. Spotify, for example, gives the artist between US$ 0.006 to US$ 0.0084 per stream, according to CNBC.

Contract deals that involve the distribution of music is another way of making money. Online platforms such as DistroKid, Songtradr, and TuneCore can distribute your music to major online platforms for yearly subscription fees, without taking away any of the royalties owned by the recording artist. This is good because, in the past, the distribution of music could only be achieved through the help of a record label. The middle man has now been cut off, and recording artists are now able to make money from their work.

Merchandising products, touring, live shows, and product placements are lucrative ways for recording artists to make money from their music. However, to do so, they need to partner with other entrepreneurs who are not involved in music-making but play a major role in the music industry. These are recording artist managers, music lawyers, and record labels.

Recording artist manager

A recording artist manager is responsible for managing the day-to-day and long-term professional activities of recording artists. Known within the music industry as a manager, their scope of work varies depending on the requirements of the client, and the size and level of the client's career. Their role includes:

- A publicist who is responsible for generating media attention and managing public relations for the recording artist.
- A business manager who is responsible for managing the artist's financial affairs.
- A music agent who is responsible for booking the artist's live shows and personal appearances.

Music lawyer

A music lawyer is an entertainment lawyer who represents people working within the music industry. Their role is to act on behalf of the recording artists, in negotiating and drafting contracts with record labels and for live performances.

Record label

A record label or record company is an enterprise that markets recorded music and any additional work produced by a recording artist. It is responsible for overseeing and incorporating all aspects of the work done by the recording artist's manager and music lawyer. It also conducts additional functions that include A&R (Artists and Repertoire) which is discovering and recruitment of promising new talent, as well as music distribution.

The music industry, just like other industries, functions through having the input of different moving parts which complement each other. One may think that making music is a simple process, but this is far from the truth. The amount of collaboration and work that goes into getting a song from the studio to various listening platforms such as radio, TV, YouTube, or Spotify is a tall order.

What it Takes to Succeed as a Music Entrepreneur

As we have seen, the music industry is wide and there are many opportunities for entrepreneurs to operate. For you to succeed as an entrepreneur within the music industry you need to:

- Have a good understanding of the industry so that you know where you fit in.
- Once you identify your market niche, stay in touch with the latest trends so that you can be relevant to be able to survive.
- Understand the local and global music industry laws to avoid lawsuits.
- Know how to use social media to promote and market your talent and skills.
- Form strategic partnerships and collaborations with other players within the industry. This will help you to expand your ideas, experience, and exposure. It will also help you to gain access to resources that you would not be able to access if you work in isolation.

Fashion Industry

Fashion is the language of human expression. What we wear says a lot about who we are, or who we aspire to be. Every day, we come face-to-face with fashion, be it in clothing, footwear, or accessories.

The fashion industry is among the largest creative industries around the world. It is a source of income for many people working within the value chain that includes designers, manufacturers, wholesalers, and vendors. The industry is very competitive, as it is dominated by the presence of many local and international entrepreneurs.

Entrepreneurs operating within the fashion industry cater to a large population from babies to youth, middle-aged and old people. This gives them the leeway of being as creative and innovative as they can, to meet the ever-increasing demand for clothes, footwear, and accessories.

Opportunities within the Fashion Industry

The fashion industry is divided into four levels. The first level is the production of raw material, which includes mills and yarn makers. The second level has designers, manufacturers, wholesalers, and vendors. The third level is retail, which has all types of stores and distribution points for sale. The fourth level, also known as the auxiliary level because it connects all these levels, has the press, advertising, research agencies, consultants, and fashion forecasters, who play a part in the merchandise progression to the end customer.

Since the fashion industry is wide, and this book aims to highlight ways of making money using your talent, we will focus on the fashion designer for clothes, footwear, and accessories.

Fashion Designers

Fashion designers design ready-to-wear clothes. They also design footwear, and accessories such as bags, and belts.

Some fashion designers prefer to work independently. This means that they are in charge of purchasing materials for designs, as well as for deciding how to price and market their work. Other designers sell their services to individuals, private labels, and merchandising companies.

When setting up a business as a fashion designer, the first step is to identify your market niche. For example, if you deal with clothes and footwear, some of the options to consider are casual clothes, formal wear, sportswear, or celebrity-endorsed wear. Once this is done, you need to identify the market segment you want to serve, which comprises men, women, unisex, or children's wear. You then need to identify your selling point—which is the value you are selling to your customers. Is it speed, innovation, or quality of your products?

When setting up a business as a fashion designer, the first step is to identify your market niche.

Last but not least, you need to package the value you are selling in a way that effectively communicates to your customers. This will help your customers to differentiate your products from what your competitors are offering.

It is important to know your market niche so that you can focus on producing what you know your customers want. If you do not know your market niche, you face the danger of producing products that nobody wants to buy.

Martha is one of the most organized fashion designers I have ever met. She runs her business from her house, where the garage has been converted into an office cum work area. I first met Martha when I was part of the bridal party during my cousin's wedding, and all our gowns were made by her. After this, I became her regular customer. When you walk into her workstation, things are well placed on the shelves, and each shelf has a label describing the contents.

What distinguishes Martha from most fashion designers I know is the fact that she not only works with individuals, but she also works with corporates. Her breakthrough came one day when she got a big order to make staff uniforms for an international hotel. Since then, her business has grown, and she has hired fashion designers to work in her team.

Doing Business as a Fashion Designer

Customers within the fashion industry love to see new and different products now and then. This ends up putting a lot of pressure on fashion design entrepreneurs, who are forced to keep coming up with new ideas and collections within a short period of time.

To survive and stay in business, fashion design entrepreneurs need to be creative, and most importantly, they should be able to respond fast enough to meet the customers' expectations. Those who cannot keep up face the danger of going out of business.

The survival of the business depends on how you brand your products. Branding helps you achieve your business objectives as your target market is able to identify and buy your products. Your brand reflects who you are and what your products aim to achieve. Should you realize that your brand is not doing well in the market, you need to have the flexibility to re-brand. It will help you keep up with the new changes taking place in the business market.

Fashion design entrepreneurs need to constantly familiarize themselves with the latest fashion trends. They have to develop a habit of learning, and there are a lot of resources that provide information and knowledge on how to keep up with the fashion industry. These are magazines, YouTube, books, or by following fashion influencers on social media channels.

Fashion design entrepreneurs need to constantly familiarize themselves with the latest fashion trends.

As a fashion design entrepreneur, you need to know what your local and international competitors are doing—and what they are not doing—then see where you can fit in and how you can challenge yourself to do better than them.

Fashion design entrepreneurs need to have a social media strategy and presence to market their products. This means that they have to choose what will work best for them. The main options available are Instagram, Facebook, Pinterest, Snapchat, and Twitter.

Staying connected with customers is important in building brand loyalty for your products. To do this successfully, appoint someone responsible for engaging with followers on your social media accounts.

What it Takes to Succeed as a Fashion Design Entrepreneur

The most important thing to understand as a fashion design entrepreneur is that creativity alone is not enough to succeed. You also need to think, prepare and make decisions. In addition, you need to stay relevant in the fashion industry by:

- Knowing the type of clothes, footwear, or accessories to make
- Producing something unique
- Identifying the market for your products
- Putting the right price for your products
- Believing in yourself to succeed
- Having customers who support you

Customers in the fashion industry buy what is relevant, new, and fresh. This means that if you want to stay in business as a fashion design entrepreneur, you have to keep an account of your progress. Doing this will help you stay relevant, not only to yourself but to your customers as well. You also need to create suspense in your customers so that they are conditioned to wait in anticipation for your next creation. By being consistent, you will keep your existing customers, and as the word goes around, you will get new ones.

Visual Arts Industry

Visual arts are any form of skill that is visual in nature. It includes graphic design, crafts, ceramics, sculpture, painting, drawing, installations, interior design, as well as video and film production, among others. Visual arts play an important role in society by allowing people from different backgrounds and cultures to communicate with each other through images.

Entrepreneurs operating within the visual arts industry know the importance of creating memorable experiences around their products. This in turn creates a lifestyle for their customers.

Since the visual arts industry is wide, and it encompasses different types of talents and skills, we will focus on painting, graphic design, and crafts to highlight ways of making money using your talent. But the same principle can also be applied to the other fields previously mentioned.

Painting artists

Gone are the days when painting artists struggled to sell their work. Things have now changed and people are appreciating art more, which has increased opportunities for artists to make money from their creativity. However, the challenge for many painting artists is that they do not have an entrepreneurial mindset.

One way of developing an entrepreneurial mindset as a paint artist is by networking with other artists and people who buy art. It is through interacting with these people that you will get to learn more about the market needs and requirements, and how to price your work.

Once you develop an entrepreneurial mindset, you will have clarity on the type of work to produce and sell. That will be appealing to the customers. Another way of making money is by teaching. You could opt to open an art school, which does not have to be big, or simply conduct one on one lessons.

Selling high-quality prints of your paintings is another way of making money. This is a good avenue of opening doors for your fans who may not be able to afford the price of the original pieces. Selling high-quality prints of your paintings also allows you to diversify the type of customers and collectors you attract.

Graphic designer

The demand for creative and reliable graphic designers is on the rise. This means that graphic designers who want to start their businesses have the opportunity of providing services to marketers and advertisers who are looking for eye-catching and informative graphics, for online and social media communication.

To start as a self-employed graphic designer, find organizations that want to produce designs for logos, magazines, newsletters, book layouts, greeting cards, and other communication materials. Photo editing, creating cartoons, and illustrations are additional ways of making money as a graphic designer.

Some years ago, the organization I worked for needed to produce a children's magazine. The idea was to produce a colourful communication tool that was informative and entertaining for children between the age of twelve to sixteen. To produce the magazine, we had to work with a graphic designer, and this is how I met Benja, a freelance graphic designer who specializes in creating illustrations. His work was to create images and to do the design and layout of the magazine using computer software.

As a freelance graphic designer, Benja is self-employed, and he offers his services to individuals and corporates. He mostly works from home or at a coffee shop. It gives him the flexibility to do other things without being constricted in an eight-to-five office job.

The demand for visual communication services is on the rise. People are always on the lookout for graphic designers like Benja, who can produce work that draws customer's attention to what they are offering or promoting in the market.

Another opportunity for making money as a graphic designer is starting a custom design business for t-shirts and merchandise items such as key holders, mugs, stickers, and coasters, among other items. All you need to get started is a superb design to create a fan base in the market.

Graphic designers have to create a good portfolio of their work. The portfolio should demonstrate your ability to do a good job before you even meet the prospective clients to negotiate and secure a contract.

Crafts artists

People like to buy unique items made from textile, glassware, and other functional pieces that are created by crafts artists. These include handmade furniture pieces, jewellery, household objects, and other products.

It takes creativity to succeed as a crafts artist-entrepreneur. It means that you have to create unique items that people will find appealing. You also need to ensure that your products are affordable and accessible to your customers.

`Crafts artists need to constantly seek feedback from their customers and also be keen on what is happening around them. By doing so, they will be in a good position to keep revising and upgrading their products based on emerging market trends.

There is a market for selling souvenirs and gift items near my home that only opens on Saturdays. A stall run by a young man who sells handmade leather sandals decorated with beadwork is my favourite. I like it because the owner allows his customers to give him images of the design they want, to custom-make their sandals.

Allowing customers to have the freedom of choosing the design they want gives the young man advantage over his competitors. It is because he is able to produce a wide selection of designs, which he takes photos of and posts on his social media account to promote his work. Unlike his competitors, who only focus on making what they think will sell, the young man has many customers from all walks of life.

The Business Side of Visual Arts

Visual arts entrepreneurs know that the only thing standing between them and their success is their customers. This is why it is important for them to focus on increasing the number of customers on a daily basis.

Without new and repeat customers, visual arts entrepreneurs are not able to sell their products, and it becomes difficult for their businesses to survive. The solution for them is to create demand for their products so that they can sell to customers.

Before setting up your business as a visual arts entrepreneur, you first need to conduct research to identify your market niche. This will guide you to know for whom you are making your products.

Once this is done, your next move is to promote your products so that you can sell them. In other words, you need to market your products, and one of the cheapest and fastest places to do so is on social media. To get started, open a social media account and create time to regularly update it with photos and new posts of your products. Soon you will begin to increase the number of people who know about you and your products, and gradually, you will begin to sell and make money.

Networking with people within the visual arts industry is important in helping you to get your name known and marketing your products.

What it Takes to Succeed as a Visual Arts Entrepreneur

Visual arts entrepreneurs know that they have to use their creativity to start and run a successful business. To keep their customers happy, they have to ensure that their products do not run out of stock. To do this, they have to ensure that they always have a collection of completed products at hand, as they continue to produce new ones regularly. In addition to this, for you to stay in business as a visual arts entrepreneur, you need to:

- Create a signature style that will differentiate your work from others.
- Understand the buying habits of your customers.
- Know the price your customers are willing to pay for your products.
- Know where, when, and how often your customers are willing to buy.

- Believe in yourself to succeed.
- Have buying customers.

The most important thing for visual arts entrepreneurs to understand is that the ideas behind their work and products are what they are putting out in the market for people to buy.

Essential Internal Factors That Lead to Success

Success in business depends on factors that come from outside of you, also known as external factors such as capital, location, and equipment, among others. It also depends on factors that come from inside of you, also known as internal factors such as habits, positive attitudes, and beliefs, among others.

The reason most businesses collapse is because entrepreneurs put more emphasis on external factors, and overlook internal factors. There has to be a balance between these two for the business to succeed.

External factors are quite straightforward to grasp. But when it comes to internal factors, we need to be intentional in applying them when setting up and running a business. To do this, we need to adopt the following competencies:

- Have good time management skills. This will enable you to organize and plan how to divide your time when implementing different tasks. When you perfect the art of good time management, you will get more done in less time, even when time is tight and you are working under pressure. Simply put, you will work smarter and not harder.
- Prepare for each task beforehand. Doing this will place you at an advantage so that instead of being reactive to problems that come your way, you will manage the problems faster and efficiently in a proactive manner. This is because you would have had a chance to think through any potential problems and how to address them.
- Have patience. Did you know that being impatient with yourself is equivalent to self-sabotage? Yes, it is. You end up looking desperate and people will avoid you, and worse still,

you might start thinking of quitting. Patience on the other hand is a virtue that develops your skills and talents, and it also enables you to learn from your failures, as well as to remain calm even when the going gets tough. With patience, you will soldier on with life, knowing that good things take time.

- Have self-confidence. One of the surest ways of failing is when you try extremely hard to please everyone. The fact of life is that critics will always be there whether you like it or not. So, the best thing to do is to ignore people who try to put you down or to demoralize you. It is important to focus on what you have set your mind on, to prove them wrong and surround yourself with people who encourage and support you.

The good thing about internal factors is that they are free and easy to learn and acquire. Above all, the more you practice, the better you become.

Reflection

The creatives industry has many channels for making money. Where do you fit in?

____

Why do you think you will succeed?

____

____

____

____

2

Meet the Sharp Entrepreneur

Information is power. Particularly when the competition ignores the opportunity to do the same*—Mark Cuban, Entrepreneur and Investor*

The journey of an entrepreneur begins with having an idea, then turning that idea into a product. It goes to show that each entrepreneur is unique from the other without even trying. They all choose to follow their instincts, pursue what they are passionate about, and forge their path.

Entrepreneurs come from different walks of life, and no rule defines who can and who cannot be an entrepreneur. Some did not go to college, others did not graduate, while others graduated. But one thing is certain, they all have a strong belief that there is a solution to everything, and all they need to do is find, package, and sell the solution.

There are two types of entrepreneurs, lifestyle entrepreneurs, and sharp entrepreneurs. Both are driven by a desire of wanting to achieve independence in controlling their destiny and making money. The difference between these two is that lifestyle entrepreneurs focus on generating money to maintain a certain way of life, and do not concern themselves with building businesses that can survive without them. In other words, they prefer to operate in a way that they are personally involved in every aspect of the business.

Sharp entrepreneurs are driven by the desire to grow their businesses to a level that does not require their day-to-day intervention. This means that they think big and long term, and make smart decisions when it comes to taking risks and seizing opportunities. They also capitalize on existing opportunities. Their focus is on maximizing the use of their talent or seizing the opportunity to apply new technology—to start a business. From a financial point of view, sharp entrepreneurs want to make money by growing and expanding their businesses.

Choosing the Right Fit

One of the best ways of becoming a sharp entrepreneur is being able to identify the different types of entrepreneurs that exist. Having this knowledge will give you an idea of what is suitable for you, based on your personality and environment, and most importantly, the available resources.

Go-getter entrepreneurs

These types of entrepreneurs usually start small with whatever resources they have, with the aim of growing their businesses as time goes by. They are goal-oriented, self-driven, and work extra hard to attain their goals.

Innovator entrepreneurs

These types of entrepreneurs are gifted in coming up with new ideas, which they turn into viable businesses. They are passionate about what they do and never lose sight of their vision until they complete the task at hand.

Imitator entrepreneurs

These types of entrepreneurs are very good at copying what other businesses are doing—but go a step farther to make improvements. They are always on the lookout for ways of having an upper hand in the market by adding value to existing products and services.

Investor entrepreneurs

These types of entrepreneurs have money. They specialize in identifying and acquiring viable businesses or assets, then hire people to run and grow them on their behalf. They know when and where to invest; they always have an exit strategy.

I don't know anyone else who is as ambitious as my friend Lily. When we were in college, she used to buy t-shirts and use screen print to decorate then sell them to students. Like most go-getter entrepreneurs, she made good money from selling her product to many customers.

As time went by, sales of the t-shirts started going down; Lily decided to venture into a different business to sell Ankara branded denim jeans and jackets. This was after she heard from people that Ankara branded items were popular among the youth. Within a short time, Lily had graduated from a go-getter entrepreneur to an imitator entrepreneur.

After completing college, Lily used her talent to paint to open a garage for drawing graffiti art on passenger-carrying vehicles, something that is popular in my country. She is now an innovator entrepreneur who creates unique graffiti art designs on vehicles.

What it Takes to be a Sharp Entrepreneur

A sharp entrepreneur's personal and business goals are intertwined. This means that they build their business to fulfil personal goals, an indication that it takes more than just having big ideas to become a sharp entrepreneur. Below are some key qualities of sharp entrepreneurs that help them to successfully set up and run their businesses.

Goal-oriented

Sharp entrepreneurs are determined to make their businesses succeed and will remove anything that stands in their way. They are very strategic and always have a clear picture of what they want to achieve—and how to go about it.

Commitment

Sharp entrepreneurs never give up. They view failure as an opportunity to learn new ways of doing things, and they will keep trying repeatedly until they succeed.

Action-oriented

Sharp entrepreneurs are proactive and know that if something needs to be done, they should do it. In as much as they are thinkers, they are also doers who focus on results and view the business as an extension of who they are.

On the lookout

Sharp entrepreneurs are always seeking new opportunities. They are good at looking at everything around them, with the aim of finding new opportunities that can be integrated into their businesses.

Passionate

This is one of the most important qualities of sharp entrepreneurs. They genuinely love what they do and are willing to go the extra mile to make the business successful.

These are some of the key qualities of a sharp entrepreneur. You may be wondering whether it is possible to possess all these qualities and more. Initially, probably not. But, with time, any entrepreneur who wants to survive in a competitive market, needs to have these qualities.

Can Anyone be an Entrepreneur?

People differ, and it is for this reason that they begin their first entrepreneurial journey at different stages of life. For some, it takes a lot of time to plan and execute the idea. For others, it just takes having the right idea—at the right time before they take off as entrepreneurs.

Anyone can be an entrepreneur. All it takes is the ability to create a new business and the determination to bear the risks that come with it, knowing that you will enjoy the rewards in the long run.

Stages of Setting up a Business

Now that we know who is an entrepreneur and the types of entrepreneurs that exist, we need to look at the stages of forming a business. It is important to understand this aspect so that as you start your business, you will be able to measure your efforts and adjust where necessary. It also helps you to visualize possible threats and opportunities to help you plan how to respond.

The sole purpose of setting up a business is to succeed, but sometimes things do not go as planned. When this happens, in most cases, it is not because of the entrepreneur's lack of resources or skills but due to a lack of understanding of the various stages of starting a business. It is like playing golf without knowing the rules and techniques for swinging a club to hit the ball so that you can get it into the hole.

Having a good understanding of the various stages of starting a business, will enable you to plan and make informed operational and financial decisions—which in turn has a direct and positive impact on the success of your business.

Chances of running a successful business reduce when the entrepreneur does not understand the stages of setting up a business.

An entrepreneur who understands the different stages of setting up a business is in a better position of knowing exactly what to do when faced with challenges.

A new business goes through three initial stages during formation, which, if well executed, puts the entrepreneur in a winning position of running a viable business. These stages are idea, initiate, and flourish. A fourth stage that most people don't like to talk about is their exit. Exiting the market is an option to consider, especially when there is a huge decline in sales, profits, and cash flow.

Idea stage

The focus at this stage is on matching your talents, skills, and passion—with the business idea you have. To do this, you need to develop a business design or model that will guide you to identify the customers you are targeting and what you have to do for your business to survive. A worksheet to help you to develop the design of your business is provided in part three of this book.

It is at this stage that you also need to determine all the resources you will need to set up your business. These include the starting capital, a place to work from, and choosing a name for your business. In addition, you also need to register your business to make it legal to protect your brand, get a license and permit to operate your business and open a business bank account. It is important to separate your personal and business accounts so that you can know if you are making a profit or not. More details on this are covered in chapter six.

You also need to figure out how to price your products and the type of relationship you want to have with your customers.

Initiate stage

This is the exciting stage for entrepreneurs because it is at this point that they start producing their products and selling to the initial customers.

The focus during this stage is on increasing the number of customers on a daily basis and creating awareness of your business and products. More details on how to get people to know and buy your products are provided in chapter five.

It is advisable to conduct a reality check now and then to find out if your business is on the right track. One way of doing this is by asking customers to give you feedback about your products and what can be improved. Failure to do this will make it difficult for you to smoothly transition to the next stage.

Should things not go as expected at this stage, and you feel like your business is not picking, your best option is to go back to the drawing board. Find out what is not working well and adjust.

Do not be afraid to start all over again because the second, third, or even fourth time around—you will be better, wiser, and well informed to make it work.

Flourish stage

When you get to this stage, it means that your idea has evolved into a business, and your sales revenue and the number of customers has steadily increased.

On the other hand, you will also begin to attract stiff competition for customers from your competitors. For you to stay in business, you have two options to consider. The first one is to get feedback from your customers to improve the product and the experience of buying from you. For instance, if you get feedback from your customers that they want the finished product to be packaged and delivered in a certain way, make it happen if it is within your ability to do so. The second option is to diversify your products into a new market with the aim to increase sales revenue. For example, if you have only been selling your product within your neighbourhood, expand to other areas. The more you sell, the bigger you become as a business and a brand.

Exit stage

Any business that fails to adapt to the changing business environment will lose its competitive advantage and will be forced to exit the market. In most cases, sales decline is an indication of a business not being able to continue to exist.

Another reason for exiting the market could be that although your business is successful, you want to venture into a new market or simply want to do something different.

A couple of years ago, I was surprised when my friend Susan, the owner of a company that produced office and home decoration materials, told me that she was selling her business. The reason I was surprised was her business doing so well. She had more than ten employees and many clients.

Her reason for selling the business was because she wanted to do something different since she was tired of doing the same thing day in and day out. Susan and her husband had bought a big piece of land where they were going to set up a dairy farm.

There are many lessons to be learned in the journey of setting up a business. That is why it is important to understand the stages of forming a business as this will enable you to know when things are going as planned and when they are not. This means that should you encounter any obstacles while setting up your business, you will be in a better position of making the necessary adjustments to be able to stay on course.

When making decisions at each stage of the business formation, it is important to follow your gut feeling, then apply the most practical solution based on your surroundings and environment.

How to Keep the Business Running During Hard Times

What comes first, being an entrepreneur or setting up a business? The answer is both because none can exist without the other, and the best way of getting better as an entrepreneur when setting up a business is to get as much information as you can about your venture. Information gives us the power to make the right decisions, especially when it comes to setting up a business.

It takes hard work, patience, and focus to successfully go through the three stages of setting up a business. For you to stay in business, you need to:

- Constantly be aware of changes taking place within the environment so that you can make adjustments in your business design where necessary. If this is not done, you stand to lose what you have worked so hard to build.
- The biggest test for most business start-ups is managing the cash flow. Cash flow is the movement of money into or out of the business. Cash flow becomes a problem when the money going out is more than the money coming in. Businesses that are likely to survive are those that figure out how to operate at a loss until the situation gets better. Some

ways of surviving the cash flow crunch include offering value for money. For example, selling two items for the price of one or offering three different products at the same price. When you pack more value into your products, customers tend to stop viewing your offer as an expense and start acknowledging the savings they are making.

- If money is not coming in and your business is operating at a loss, you need to review the demand for your products to know what is moving fast and what is not. Once you do this, stop the production of products with the lowest demand, those that generate the least revenue—and increase the production of what is popular with your customers.

The truth of the matter is that many start-up businesses go through seasons when they have to continue operating, even when they are not making money. Businesses that are likely to survive are those that figure out how to operate at a loss until the situation improves.

The Link Between the Business and the Entrepreneur

The entrepreneurial journey is not easy. Many people set up businesses with a lot of excitement, which dies soon after for different reasons. To keep going and succeeding in business, a sharp entrepreneur should have a proactive mindset.

A proactive mindset is the ability to prepare for something before it happens. This then puts you in a position of constantly focusing on finding solutions for your business by planning and taking the necessary action. It also gives you the ability to focus on doing what is within your control, instead of wasting time worrying about what you are unable to do.

When the going gets tough, having a proactive mindset helps entrepreneurs to take a stand in separating emotions from values. For example, a sharp entrepreneur will apply his proactive mindset to stay focused on his vision, even when facing discouragement and receiving negative comments from people.

Reflection

What type of entrepreneur are you or would you like to be?

____

Which qualities of an entrepreneur do you already have, and which ones do you need to acquire?

____

____

____

____

3

Using Self-leadership to Set the Business in Motion

Ambition is the path to success. Persistence is the vehicle you arrive in.*— Bill Bradley, American politician, and former professional basketball player.*

In chapter one, we learned how you could use your talent and skills to make money. In the following chapter, we learned that the first step of setting up a business is knowing which type of entrepreneur you are, based on your personality and environment, and most importantly, the available resources. What follows is understanding what self-leadership is, and the important role it plays in shaping your success as an entrepreneur.

Leadership, in general, is about how someone influences others, but when it comes to self-leadership, it is about observing and managing yourself. Self-leadership is the act of having a good sense of who you are, what you can do, where you are going, and how you will get there. It is having a clear and accurate understanding of your potential to undertake a task or project, and knowing how to make amendments in your areas of weakness.

Entrepreneurs who are aware of their self-leadership skills have a competitive advantage over others. Self-leadership gives them the ability to build a strong foundation for their businesses, making them highly effective and productive.

Role of Self-Leadership in Entrepreneurial Success

Self-leadership skills give you the ability to seize opportunities within the market because you become more assertive, decisive, and confident when discharging your authority on matters related to your business.

Self-leadership is an important trait to have when developing an entrepreneurial mindset. This is because it enables you to have control over how to plan, implement, and attain your goals. Other benefits of self-leadership are:

- You take full responsibility for your actions or lack of acting.
- You become more efficient and productive.
- You get inspired to act.
- You build strong relationships with the people you interact with.
- You convince others to follow your lead in doing business with you.

Anyone can be an entrepreneur, so long as the person has a business idea and knows how it would be rolled out. When a former colleague of mine got fired from his job, he knew for sure that it was time for him to set up a business so that he had the independence and freedom of following his passion. Jack loved making household furniture pieces, and he was good at it. He discovered his talent one day when he made seats for his garden. Before long, he had made a kitchen seating bench for his house that he ended up selling to a friend of his who loved it. Most of the furniture pieces in his house were made by him.

So, when Jack got fired from his job, he decided to turn his garage into a workstation. He didn't have to buy a lot of equipment since he already had what he needed. With his savings, Jack bought materials and started his business. Today, he is one of the most sorted-after furniture carpenters that interior designers work with.

Jack attributes his success to being assertive in following his passion for making furniture pieces, as well as being decisive in learning as much as he could about what it takes to start and run a business. The knowledge he gained helped him to make clear-cut and timely decisions concerning his business. Having confidence helped him package himself well, and that is how he ended up doing business with interior designers instead of waiting for walk-in customers. Being assertive and decisive, and having confidence, enabled Jack to begin the journey to becoming an entrepreneur from a winning position.

How to Develop Self-Leadership Skills

It takes practice and time to learn self-leadership skills, but the rewards are worth it. There are four steps, when put together, form the concept of self-leadership. These are:

Step I: Discover who you really are

Everyone has beliefs and values that shape the way they view life and conduct themselves.

By discovering who you are, what is important to you, what energizes you, and what you think about money when it comes to doing business—makes it easy for you to have confidence when making important decisions about your business.

Step II: Accept who you are

Accepting who you are, makes it less stressful to admit the truth of the matter, especially when things are not going as planned, which then helps you to make the necessary changes. It also helps you to focus on what really matters to you, while being comfortable with where you are right now, knowing that things will soon get better.

Accepting who you are, helps in making important decisions. This is because you become realistic with yourself, to accept what you are capable of doing—and what you are not able to do—that you need to delegate, for your business to succeed.

Step III: Manage your time well

Whoever said that time waits for no man knew exactly what it meant to waste time and miss opportunities. When you manage your time well, you become more productive and focused on attaining your business goals.

Managing your time well is not about overworking or pushing yourself too hard. It is about planning and prioritizing your activities in a way that gives you control and a good balance in what you are doing.

Step IV: Make personal growth and development a priority

One way of improving your problem-solving skills is to be intentional in learning something new every day. To do this, make it a habit to be curious by asking questions and learning as much as you can about your industry. This will help you to close any knowledge gaps you may be having, which then makes you more professional and competent.

How to Improve Self-Leadership Skills

Self-leadership helps you to become aware of your true talent and the vision you have for your life. When it comes to setting up a business, self-leadership helps you to be intentional in developing an entrepreneurial mindset. You can improve your self-leadership skills by answering the following questions.

- What is my talent—something that I enjoy doing?
- What am I doing with my life—and is it something I enjoy doing?
- What would I rather be doing with my life—but keep pushing the idea away?
- When I think of what I would rather be doing with my life—do I formulate a vision for my life?

- Does my vision make me feel motivated to act—to create something new, find a solution to a problem, or change the status quo?

Self-leadership makes you a better communicator, more creative, a critical thinker, and good at collaborating with others. All these qualities will help you to build the foundation of becoming a successful person and entrepreneur. When it comes to developing an entrepreneurial mindset, self-leadership plays a big role in helping you to get better results from your business.

For you to excel as an entrepreneur, you need to improve your self-leadership skills. Doing this will enable you to be more intentional when setting and implementing your business goals.

Strategies of Staying on the Right Track

A sharp entrepreneur is strategic in setting up and running the business by focusing on key activities that will lead to the attainment of set goals. Being strategic helps the entrepreneur to keep a track of the progress being made. It also gives the entrepreneur the flexibility of realigning ongoing activities with changes taking place in the market.

For you to stay on the right track while setting up and running your business, you need to set realistic and attainable goals. You also need to develop and implement an activity plan of what needs to be done, how it would be done, and by when it would be done. Success in business takes time, dedication, and hard work.

Next, you need to set your standards. Do not judge yourself according to other people's definition of success. Instead, decide from the onset what is most important to you while setting up your business—then set an indicator that you will use to measure progress. For example, you could decide that you want to have 10 customers within the first three months of starting your business. This is more attainable compared to wanting to have 1000 customers within the same period.

Lastly, develop a bounce-back strategy. It is normal to face occasional roadblocks along the way—and it happens to all of us. This means that it is important to train yourself to treat every obstacle as a learning lesson. Should things not go as planned, make adjustments and try again.

The end result of being strategic is that you will be more focused and patient in getting your businesses where you see them in the near future.

Reflection

What are you good at doing when working on a new project?
□Creativity/ideas □Planning/organizing
□Implementing/execution □Others

What do you need to do to get better at what you do?

____

____

____

What is your weakness when starting/working on a new project? □ Getting started □ Maintaining the momentum □ Completing what I start □ Meeting deadlines

What do you need to do to overcome this challenge?

____

____

____

PART TWO

THE MONEY SIDE OF DOING BUSINESS

4

Creating a Competitive Advantage

Ideas are worth nothing unless executed. They are just a multiplier. Execution is worth millions.*— Steve Jobs, business magnate, industrial designer, and investor.*

Starting a business is the easy part, but keeping the business running is the tough part. Yes, you have produced your product, but what happens when it does not sell?

The sharp entrepreneur knows that if the business does not sell its products, it will not survive. The solution is to have a competitive advantage that distinguishes the business from its competitors.

A business that creates a competitive advantage is able to get more customers and earn more money. It is also able to create brand loyalty.

Establishing a competitive advantage is one of the most important objectives of any entrepreneur. Think of it this way; every time you produce and sell your products, you compete in a highly competitive market where others offer similar products. For this reason, it is important to add something 'extra' to your products so that your customers can easily recognize them as more superior compared to what your competitors are offering. So, the question posed by the sharp entrepreneur is: How can I improve my products so that customers can see the value over what my competitors are offering?

To address this, a sharp entrepreneur knows that before producing a product, it is important to add value that will make it stand out from what already exists in the market. The two ways of going about this are product improvement or product innovation.

When Sifa started his cooking business, he opened a food stall near a university, but after some time, he realized that the orders were not fast-moving. So, he decided to get feedback from his customers, and from the findings, he learned that the students wanted to be served big portions of healthy lunch meals and different varieties of snacks. He later improved his menu, and as a result, the number of customers at his food stall increased by a big margin.

Once a business is up and running, it is important to always make a follow up with customers to get feedback on the products provided. This helps the entrepreneur to keep making improvements that would help the business to grow, just like Sifa's did.

Product Improvement

Product improvement simply means to add value. It is implemented when a change is made to a product that already exists in the market. The incentive of using this approach is to meet the ever-changing market demands, or in reaction to innovation that a competitor had previously introduced into the market—but is lacking in certain aspects that will make it function better.

Improvement is copying a product or service that exists but adding some value to it.

Product Innovation

Product innovation is much more. It is the creation of a new product in the market. It is about creating a superior economic return product or service that competitors are not able to match.

Innovation can take the form of introducing to the market, a new process of doing something, a new product that changes the way people live, or a new business design that changes the way an organization functions.

Product Improvement vs. Product Innovation: Making the choice

Sharp entrepreneurs who position themselves to either embrace product improvement or product innovation are the ones who survive in today's competitive business market.

Choosing the product improvement approach begins by asking; "How can I run my business better than my competitors?" The answer enables the entrepreneur to know what to do and make gradual changes that will make the products better than what is being offered by the competitors. Some product improvement options to consider are:

- Improve the quality of your products. Quality is what customers perceive as an added value of your products. Find out what your customers want, and provide faster than your competitors.
- Provide expert advice through your social media accounts. You can add value by providing expert advice on the benefits of buying your products. By doing this, you will create a personalized customer experience that will increase brand loyalty for your products.
- Improve design and packaging of products. The first thing customers see and feel is the design and packaging of your products. This has a direct impact on whether or not they will buy your products. To influence their decision-making in relation to buying your products, you need to have an attractive design and packaging of your products.
- Improve customer service and experience to increase the number of repeat customers. A quality product is the first part of getting customers to buy from you. Next, you need to entice them to choose to do business with you over your

competitors who provide similar or even cheaper products. Some ways of improving customer service include responding promptly to inquiries and making a follow-up after a product has been sold, to find out if the customer had a good experience during the purchasing process. You can also provide discount coupons to customers to communicate the notion that the more someone buys from you, the more value for money they get for items purchased.

Should you choose to apply the product innovation approach, one way of going about this is to design and develop new products that provide creative solutions in solving people's problems. The other way of being innovative and making the products stand out from the rest is to develop a unique signature style. For example, an artist could have a signature of painting people with 'square shaped head'. With time, people will distinguish the painter's work from what other painters are doing.

Product Improvement vs. Product Innovation: The Application

Product improvement is much easier to implement compared to product innovation. This is because product improvement gives you the flexibility of making improvements to existing products. For example, you could improve the production by modifying the quantity or quality of materials used, or simply by making the best use of resources to maximize profit.

One of the limitations of applying the product improvement approach is that any improvement you make can also be copied by someone else. So, it is safe to always think of this approach as something that gives you a temporary advantage before someone else comes up with new ways of making additional improvements to the same product.

The product innovation approach is not easy, but the rewards are great in boosting the productivity, growth, and profitability of the business. Whatever form it takes, product innovation is a creative process that involves filtering new ideas and identifying those that the entrepreneur will roll out.

One way of identifying opportunities for innovation is through adjusting your products to fit within the changes taking place in the market. For example, if people are increasingly working from home, as an entrepreneur, you could develop a product that will help to make their workstation more work-friendly.

Innovation is a costly venture that requires some investment. Should you choose this option, you will need to self-fund or tap into external funding for loans.

The sharp entrepreneur is always on the lookout for ways of introducing new and improved products as a way of increasing sales revenue. Businesses that fail to act when the time comes to either improve or innovate their products, face the danger of reducing profit margins, and eventually going out of business. On the other hand, those that embrace improvement and innovation stand a better chance of improving productivity and adding value to their products, which then increases profit margins.

Consideration has to be made when choosing the right approach between product improvement and product innovation so that your business can have a competitive advantage. Choosing the right approach will not only improve customer loyalty but also enable your business to run smoothly without the fear of drastic cash flow interruptions.

Getting Feedback to Stay Relevant

Sometimes things will not go as planned when setting up and running a business. For example, your initial plan as a fashion design entrepreneur may have been to produce clothes, but with time, you realize that most of your customers are asking for interior design fashion pieces such as curtains and cushions covers. It is therefore important to have the flexibility of diversifying your products to accommodate what your customers are asking for—as you keep moving towards accomplishing your business objectives.

As an entrepreneur, you need to have the flexibility of changing with the times so that you can stay in business. It means that you should listen keenly to feedback from your customers and try your level best to meet them wholly or at least halfway. A happy customer will come back for more, and most importantly, will tell others about your products.

Not all criticism is bad. But this does not mean that you should concentrate on it. On the other hand, you should not fight it. Let your customers and competitors know that you appreciate their feedback. Once you receive feedback, evaluate what has been said, and seek a second and even third opinion. You should then learn useful lessons from the overall feedback received and make the necessary adjustments to your products. Remember, many achievers would have remained ordinary people had they not been criticized. The most successful entrepreneurs are those who are humble enough to manage criticism.

Reflection

Product improvement and product innovation are the driving force behind the success of every business. In your opinion, how does this apply in:

Business expansion.

____

____

____

Staying ahead of competitors.

____

____

____

Customer retention.

____

____

____

5

Getting People to Know and Buy Your Products

People do not buy goods and services. They buy relations, stories and magic.*— Seth Godin, entrepreneur, best-selling author, and speaker.*

Every business wants to attract customers. This means that entrepreneurs have to find ways of reaching customers, drawing their attention to the products and keeping them coming back for more.

People are more likely to buy your products if they know about them. To achieve this, entrepreneurs have to constantly invest time and resources in creating awareness and educating customers about their products. They need to implement well-planned branding and marketing efforts.

The first time I saw someone with sisterlocks, the hair looked really nice, and I wanted to do the same for myself, but never got to do it. Sisterlocks are created by forming a woven pattern using hair. The process is time-consuming, so most people prefer to have the hairdresser making their hair in the comfort of their homes. One such hairdresser is Milka, who has many clients, and all of them either got to know about her through a friend who was also her client, or a stranger who saw the hair of one of her clients and requested for her contact.

As an entrepreneur, Milka does a good job on her clients, who then become her billboard for advertising her brand. The clients then market her work by becoming the link between her and the next clients.

Branding is the promise entrepreneurs keep when they do what they say they will do. In Milka's case, by doing a good job she not only creates a good brand for her business but also builds recognition and loyalty with her clients.

Branding is who you are, while marketing is how you get people to know about your business.

Branding

Branding is the unique identity of the business that makes them stand out from competitors. It also helps the business to attract and retain loyal customers. It is what drives people to choose your business over the others.

Branding makes your business stand out to your customers, especially if they can resonate with what you do and represent. People love to be part of something, so when they find a product they like, they take pride in representing it.

A good brand will give your business free publicity. This is because when people get to know and like your products, they will want to tell their friends, family members, and others what they like about doing business with you.

Your products will get a lot of attention if your business brand stands out compared to a business that is not branded. Without proper branding, your customers will not know about your products.

As you develop your brand, remember it goes beyond the logo and choice of colours used. It is the way you communicate through your promotion and marketing materials and how your products are packaged, displayed, and delivered to the customers. Once you create a consistent look and feel for your brand, you need to stick to the choice made.

The benefit of developing a strong brand for your business is that you will reach the right target audience, and everything else will fall in place. Ensure that you create a consistent brand so that your customers are always aware and in the know about your products.

Marketing

Marketing is the process that creates your brand awareness, attracts customers, and drives sales and your business growth. It is what gets the word out for people to know about your products by connecting your business to your customers.

The first step of implementing your marketing efforts is identifying the customers you are targeting so that you can promote and sell your products to them.

As a business start-up without a big budget for marketing, social media is one of the cheapest and fastest ways for marketing and selling your products. The process of running a social media account is simple; all you need is to set up an account and post photos of your products on a regular basis. Below are steps that will guide you to successfully run a social media account to market and sell your products as an entrepreneur.

- Complete the personal details section. Remember, the objective of your account is to sell your work, so give your followers an opportunity to know you.
- Post breath-taking and creative photos that show your followers what they are missing—and what they should be buying.
- Create videos for people to watch. People love watching videos that they can share with their friends. Videos are a good way of drawing attention to your products in a way that inspires your customers to make purchases.
- Create captivating captions that will let people know of your inspirations, process, and story behind the work. This can be the tipping point for customers to click with your products emotionally and buy your work.
- Create the right hashtag to reach people who will be interested in your work.

- Consider using paid advertisements as well, to increase the number of people reached.

As your business grows, you may want to have a website and run a YouTube channel to post videos about your products. With time, you may also want to partner with influencers to endorse your products. People are more likely to buy products endorsed by influencers.

Marketing without branding will not grow your business. You need both to be able to create an identity for your business and to promote and sell your products. When your marketing efforts reinforce your brand recognition, you will get better results.

Finding Customers

It is pointless to have a good product that nobody is buying. Therefore, customer acquisition is a key component for any business if it is to survive. A sharp entrepreneur knows that customers will not find you; you have to go out there and find them if you want to run a successful business. With proper branding and effective marketing efforts, you will be able to get customers to buy your products.

Once you get customers, you also need to manage customer acquisition because sometimes customers stop buying for one reason or another. To keep the business running, customers who stop buying have to be replaced by new ones.

The first thing to do when managing customer acquisition is to know who your ideal customers are. If you sell to an organization, you need to know which department is most likely to place orders for your products, so that you can contact the right people who are also decision-makers. If you sell to individuals, determine what the customer is looking for and what the buying cycle is. It will help you to meet your customers' needs and to know whether you are selling a product that has a long buying cycle.

Next, you need to know how a typical customer will find products similar to yours. Is it through social media? If so, open social media accounts. Do they go somewhere else when they want to buy your type of products? When you know, you will be able to form partnerships to get referrals and recommendations from those sources. The feedback will help you to know how to get more customers, and also to plan ways for placing your products in locations where people you are targeting can find them. You can also use the feedback to improve your social media presence by making sure that your pages are easy to find.

Use your networks to promote your business by asking people to introduce you to their circle of friends who they think would be interested in buying your products. This is a good lead for reaching potential customers.

Placing labels on your products that contain details of your business name, telephone number, social media accounts, and website is useful. You could also give gifts to customers and prospects that contain these details. The more people have information on how to reach you, the more customers you will acquire.

How to Set Milestones for Measuring Progress

A sharp entrepreneur always has the impulse of thinking of any internal and external factors that are likely to prevent the business from succeeding. Doing this gives the entrepreneur a good understanding of what is needed in terms of who does what, resources, and setting timelines. In other words, the entrepreneur should be aware of what must be done for the business to survive, also known as setting milestones.

To set milestones for your business, you need to ask yourself these questions:

- What is likely to stop my business from making progress? By answering this question, you will be able to assess your level of commitment in doing whatever it takes to set up and run a successful business.

- If I was in a do-or-die situation and my life depended on my business succeeding, what would I do? This question will help you to take stock of your skills and knowledge in setting up and running a successful business. In other words, you will get to know your strengths so that you can put them to productive use in running your business. It also opens your eyes to acknowledge your weaknesses so that you can figure out how to learn from them and grow.
- What is working well for my competitors that I can borrow and replicate? This question will help you to seek advice and learn from others. Skills and knowledge for running a business are improved by learning and observing what the competitors are doing so that you can know what you can borrow and adapt or improve for your business.

Reflection

It is important to create a brand that your customers will recognize. What do you want your brand to stand for?

____

____

____

6

Basic Bookkeeping for Business Start-ups

Change your focus from making money to serving more people. Serving more people makes the money come in.
— Robert Kiyosaki, businessman and author

Starting a business is a good way of using your skills and talent to make money. Once the business is set up and the money starts flowing in, it is important to have a record of the money you put into the business and the money made from sales. It is known as bookkeeping.

In chapter two, we learned that when you start a business, it is important to separate a personal account from your business account so that you can know whether you are making a profit or not. It comes in handy in bookkeeping because it allows you to keep track of business expenses and sales revenue. But how exactly does operating separate personal and business accounts work?

- All business expenses are paid out of the business account.
- All personal expenses are paid out of the personal account.
- Pay yourself a salary to avoid pulling money from the business for personal use. When you pay yourself a regular salary, you will not only increase the chances of your business succeeding, but you will also become more disciplined to stick to a budget.

Good bookkeeping matters because it helps you to run your business smoothly. If you do not know the financial status of your business, you will end up making bad decisions that will affect your business. For example, if you are not up to date with your cash in and cash out records, you could end up not being able to pay your loans on time. You could also miss making investments that would have improved the performance of your business.

Basic knowledge in bookkeeping will help you keep track of business expenditures such as operations, administration, and logistics. It will also help you to keep track of money earned from sales so that you can know whether your business is making a profit or a loss.

Bookkeeping is the first part of the accounting process that involves recording and organizing the income and expenses of the business (money coming in and money going out). Unlike accounting, bookkeeping does not get into the details of interpreting financial data.

Since completing college, my friend's son has been making and selling sculptures. Most of his work is to beautify outdoor gardens and compounds at learning institutions and shopping malls. One day, he got a big order from a university that needed four big-sized sculptures of lions facing upwards to be placed at the graduation ground.

It was good business for my friend's son, but the only problem was that he needed capital to buy the required materials. When he applied for a loan at the bank, the first thing he was asked to produce was the financial records of his business. Since he had not separated his personal account from his business account, he was not able to provide information on the cash flow history of his business. His loan application was declined.

Basic Bookkeeping Tips

To get started with bookkeeping, you need to set up a good system for storing and recording all the transactions made for cash in and cash out. The following basic bookkeeping tips will guide you to manage day-to-day income and expenses records of your business.

Have a separate business and personal account

Open a new bank account for your business so that you can separate your business money from your personal money. Should you need to use your personal money to cater to business expenses, do a money transfer to the business account. When paying yourself which is very important, transfer money from your business account to your personal account.

The good practice is to make weekly or monthly transfers from one account to the other depending on your need to reduce the bank charges. The more transfers you make, the more bank charges you will incur.

Choose the right bookkeeping software

At the bare minimum, you need to have an Excel cashbook or a hand-copy cashbook. However, as the business grows, you will need to upgrade to use software with a cashbook, ledger, bank reconciliation, account receivable, and accounts payable. Most of this software can easily be exported to Excel to generate charts, graphs, and financial reports.

Organize business documents

Have a well-organized filing and archiving system for all your business transaction documents. Do not keep a box or basket full of randomly placed receipts and forms to avoid wasting time when looking for a particular document when you need it most.

The three options to consider when setting up a basic filing system for your business are; a paper system, an electronic system in the computer, and online document storage.

Learn how to read and understand bookkeeping reports

If you want to succeed in running a business, you need to be proactive in having your bookkeeping system up to date. The income statement and the balance sheet are two financial reports that you need to learn how to read and understand if you want to run a successful business.

These two reports will give you an insight into any arising issues and opportunities in the market, and will also help you analyse the status of your business. For example, if sales suddenly went down during a particular month, you will be able to tell whether it was due to complaints received for a certain product or whether it was when you increased the price of your products.

Generate monthly bookkeeping reports so that you can be keep track of high and low seasons of selling your products. It will help you to plan your production schedule, to meet the demand of your customers.

Know when it is time to hire an accountant

It can be overwhelming for a business owner to produce the products, run the business, and do the bookkeeping. When you get to the point where you are not able to cope with doing the bookkeeping, the best option is to hire an account.

The advantage of hiring an accountant is the added value that comes with it. This includes having someone who gives you sound business advice on various issues such as when to buy new software that is a good fit for your business, helping to prepare your annual budget and cash flow reports, and explaining to you any aspects of finance that you are not familiar with.

Work Smart

As we have seen, a lot of work goes into setting up and running a business. To be able to manoeuvre, a sharp entrepreneur has to work smart. Working smart simply means that you should determine what needs to be done and do it without fail. It also means that you need to put in extra effort by working out of your comfort zone in order to run a successful business.

Imagination is one of the greatest gifts that everyone has. As an entrepreneur, you need to apply your imagination to find solutions to challenges faced while setting up and running the business. It is a smart way of working that will help you make the right decisions and steer you towards attaining the objectives of your business.

Another way of working smart is asking for help. People are the best resources that anyone can have. A sharp entrepreneur knows when to ask for help from people who are doing what he is trying to do. Asking for help does not mean that you are weak. It is an indication that you are wise, and you know that on your own you will not be able to achieve much.

Reflection

Why do you think most business start-ups fail to keep proper bookkeeping records?

____

____

____

What measures will you take to ensure that your business bookkeeping records are up to date?

____

____

____

7

How to Start from a Winning Position

Don't watch the clock. Do what it does. Keep going.
— Sam Levenson, writer, teacher, television host, and journalist.

A good starting point of setting up a business is when you promise yourself to do everything within your power to succeed. This is followed by being specific about the product you want to produce. If you are producing more than one product, make sure that you have a signature product, the one that you want your business to be well known for.

The next thing to do is to ensure that you meet the legal requirements of starting a business. For example, register your business name and get a business permit.

Setting operation systems for your business at the initial stages is important and will save you a lot of headaches as the business grows. For example, you need to develop templates for invoices, delivery notes, letterheads, job cards to fill in details of your customers, and petty cash vouchers. To ensure proper use of these documents and to facilitate future reference, they should be filed in appropriate folders, either in soft copy or physical files.

Communication with potential clients is very important because it is the only way of getting your products known by your target audience. Plan in advance how you are going to create awareness of your products.

Cash flow is what makes or breaks a business. You need to know how your business will generate cash flow so that the money coming in is more than what goes out, with the exception of when buying assets for the business. Simple ways of managing the cash flow are to lease equipment instead of buying, offering discounts for early payment as a way of getting more customers, and improving your inventory so that you stock more of the fast-moving items and less of what is not in high demand.

You have to pay yourself because you have personal expenses such as paying rent and buying food by receiving a draw. A draw is taken out of the profits after paying all the business expenses. As the business grows, you may want to consider paying yourself a salary instead of receiving a draw.

At the beginning of the book, a question was posed on imagining the reality of doing business, where you could use your talent to make money. Different topics have been covered to help you get started in setting up and running a business. One thing that has come out clearly is that an entrepreneur—at the initial stages— plays the role of the visionary, the producer, the accountant, the sales manager, and wears many other hats.

To succeed in setting up a business, a sharp entrepreneur must get into a winning position of ready-set-go.

Ready

After reading the book up to this point, you are in the "ready" position, most probably. It is good because you already know what type of entrepreneur you are. You also know the talent you are going to use to make money by starting your business. You have also taken stock of your self-leadership skills and know what you are capable of achieving when setting up the business.

Set

In the "set" position, you start thinking ahead about how you are going to make your product unique and different from what your competitors are selling. What follows is knowing how you will make your product known in the market in order to acquire customers. It is a risky business to start producing your products when you do not know how you are going to get customers. To avoid this, ensure that you know the customers you are targeting and how you are will draw their attention to your product and keep them coming back for more.

You also need to plan how you will keep track of cash in and cash out as a way of knowing whether the business is making a profit or a loss.

Go

One step to take before getting into the "go" position is identifying the opportunity, the market, and the money aspects of your business. With this information, you will be able to create the design of your business. Worksheet two provided in the following pages will guide you in developing the design of your business.

Once you develop the design of your business, you will be in the winning position of take-off to become a sharp entrepreneur.

Determination and Commitment Lead to Success

In chapter two we learned that anyone can be an entrepreneur, and all it takes is having the ability to create a new business, and have the determination to bear the risks that come with it. To get started as an entrepreneur, it is important to first assess how determined and committed you are in setting up and running your business. This will help you to stay focused—especially when the going gets tough.

When setting up a business, you have to determine what is important to you, as far as being an entrepreneur is concerned. Do you want to express yourself and show the world your creative side? Do you want to be financially independent? Do you want both?

You also need to assess your level of commitment in setting up the business. This is done by making a commitment to honour what you have determined to be important to you, then plan your next course of action. You will feel inspired to do whatever it takes in setting up your business when you know how committed you are to succeeding.

The advantage of assessing your level of determination and commitment before setting up the business is that your dreams, values, and actions will be aligned. When this happens, you will be starting from the winning position of a sharp entrepreneur.

PART THREE

BUSINESS STARTUP WORKSHEETS

Take the Driver's Seat to Become a Sharp Entrepreneur

We have covered in detail the building blocks that will guide you in connecting who you are and what you do—with how you can make money using your talent. Now you need to put what you have learned into practice.

I invite you to take the driver's seat to become a sharp entrepreneur by completing worksheets 1 and 2. Each of the worksheets poses questions that prompt you to think clearly about what you want to achieve, as well as to write down your thoughts.

The first worksheet will guide you on how to develop an entrepreneurial mindset, while the second one will guide you on how to develop your business design.

After completing the two worksheets, you will have a place to refer to later, as a reminder of what you have committed to do in setting up and running your business.

Worksheet 1

How to Develop an Entrepreneurial Mindset

***The results you achieve will be in direct proportion to the effort you apply.**— Denis Waitley, Best-selling author and speaker.*

This worksheet will guide you on how to develop your business roadmap. Once completed, put a bookmark so that you can keep referring to it every day as a reminder of what you need to do to succeed as an entrepreneur.

____

The name of my business is:

____

This is what I am good at:

- ____
- ____
- ____
- ____

This is the product I want to sell:

- ____
- ____
- ____
- ____

These are the activities I will do to produce my product:

- ________________________________
- ________________________________
- ________________________________
- ________________________________

This is what it will cost me to produce the first product:

- ________________________________
- ________________________________
- ________________________________
- ________________________________

These are the customers I am targeting:

- ________________________________
- ________________________________
- ________________________________
- ________________________________

This is the kind of relationship I want to have with my customers:

- ________________________________
- ________________________________
- ________________________________
- ________________________________

This is what I must do to become a sharp entrepreneur:

- ________________________________
- ________________________________
- ________________________________
- ________________________________

Worksheet 2

My Business Design

Some people dream of success, while other people get up every morning and make it happen. — *Wayne Huizenga, Businessman and Entrepreneur.*

This worksheet will empower you with the knowledge you need to set up and run your business. By writing down your responses in each question posed, you will be able to analyse your situation, plan, and begin the journey to becoming a sharp entrepreneur.

The opportunity

The key challenge faced by many aspiring entrepreneurs is not being able to identify a business opportunity that is the right fit for them. This section will guide you on how to identify the business opportunity that is a good match for your skills and talent.

____

Which business opportunity have you identified?

- ____
- ____
- ____
- ____

How do you plan to capture the opportunity?

- ______________________________
- ______________________________
- ______________________________
- ______________________________

How will customers benefit from your product?

- ______________________________
- ______________________________
- ______________________________
- ______________________________

What is the vision for your business and how do you create it?

- ______________________________
- ______________________________
- ______________________________
- ______________________________

The Market

By knowing who you are targeting to sell to, you will be in a better position to focus on your selling, marketing and branding efforts to a specific market—that is more likely to buy from you, than from your competitors. It then becomes affordable, efficient, and an effective way of reaching potential customers to generate business. This section will guide you on how to identify your target market.

____

Which segment of customers are you targeting?

- ____
- ____
- ____
- ____

Why will your business succeed in reaching these customers?

- ____
- ____
- ____
- ____

The money

A business generates money from sales made. This means that pricing of products has a direct impact on every aspect of your business. This section will guide you on how to price your products.

What are the fixed costs of running the business?

- ____
- ____
- ____
- ____

How much will you charge—and why will customers pay the price?

- ____________________
- ____________________
- ____________________
- ____________________

How will you win customers who are willing to pay this price?

- ____________________
- ____________________
- ____________________
- ____________________

Notes

Chapter 1

1. Creativelive, 'How to become a creative entrepreneur', Suchi Rudra, 2018, https://www.creativelive.com/blog/how-to-become-a-creative-entrepreneur/
2. The balance small business, Basic principles of creative entrepreneurs, https://www.thebalancesmb.com/basic-principals-of-creative-entrepreneurs-
3. Times International, How much can you earn on Spotify? Robert Kormoczi, 2019, https://www.timesinternational.net/how-much-can-an-artist-earn-on-spotify/#:~:text=According%20to%20CNBC%2C%20artists%20can,lower%20at%20%240.00437%20per%20play.
4. The Balance Careers, The Record Label's Role in the Music Industry, Heather Mcdonald, 2019, https://www.thebalancecareers.com/what-is-a-record-label-2460614#:~:text=Record%20labels%20are%20companies%20that,music%20publishing%2C%20and%20copyright%20enforcement.
5. Berklee, Artist Manager, https://www.berklee.edu/careers/roles/artist-manager
6. The Balance Careers, What a Music Publishing Company Does, Heather Mcdonald, 2019, https://www.thebalancecareers.com/what-does-a-music-publishing-company-do-2460915
7. Study.com, How to Become a Music Engineer – Step by step Career Roadmap, 2020, https://study.com/articles/How_to_Become_a_Music_Engineer_Step-by-Step_Career_Roadmap.html
8. Artwork Archives, 'Artists as entrepreneurs: Your art is your business', Art Design Consultants, https://www.artworkarchive.com/blog/artists-are-entrepreneurs-your-art-is-your-business

9. Opinion, Why Drake is the most important artist of his generation, Rudi Kinsella, https://www.joe.ie/music/opinion-drake-important-artist-generation-589999.
10. Henna Ray, https://tdsblog.com/tips-staying-relevant-fashion-industry/ July 2017, https://www.designhill.com/design-blog/top-10-tips-on-starting-a-successful-fashion-design-business/
11. Paint and party, How does art affect culture and society?, https://www.masterpiecemixers.com/art-affect-culture-society/#:~:text=Art%20influences%20society%20by%20changing,of%20a%20society's%20collective%20memory.
12. Roth Society, Art transformed, http://rothsociety.org/the-importance-of-visual-art.htm
13. The Artic, The Death of the Artist—and the Birth of the Creative Entrepreneur, William Deresiewicz, January/February 2015, https://www.theatlantic.com/magazine/archive/2015/01/the-death-of-the-artist-and-the-birth-of-the-creative-entrepreneur/383497/
14. Business news daily, small business solutions and inspirations, Julianna Lopez, January 16, 2019, https://www.businessnewsdaily.com/5183-art-business-ideas.html
15. Spinning pots, Can I make money making pottery? 2018, https://spinningpots.com/can-i-make-money-making-pottery/
16. How to Quit Your Day Job and Pursue a Career in Ceramics, Katelan Cunningham, August 2015, https://www.brit.co/quit-you-day-job-ceramics/
17. The ceramic school, How to start a successful pottery business the right way, https://ceramic.school/how-to-start-a-successful-pottery-business/
18. Simple, How to start earning money as an artist, https://www.simple.com/blog/how-to-start-earning-money-as-an-artist

19. My modern met, Eight innovative ways to make money from your art, Jessica Stewart, March 2020, https://mymodernmet.com/how-to-make-money-from-art/
20. Artwork archive, How to make money as an artist on Instagram, https://www.artworkarchive.com/blog/how-to-make-money-as-an-artist-on-instagram
21. Your free career test, How do crafts artists sell, https://www.yourfreecareertest.com/craft-artist/Chapter 1:

Chapter 2

1. The Questions Every Entrepreneur Must Answer, Amar Bhide, 1996, Harvard Business Review, https://hbr.org/1996/11/the-questions-every-entrepreneur-must-answer
2. Entrepreneur, 'Business essentials', Adams Hayes, update in July 1, 2020, https://www.investopedia.com/terms/e/entrepreneur.asp
3. Entrepreneur, Start-up basics, 'Who is an entrepreneur', Juan Jose de la Torre, April 30, 2015, https://www.entrepreneur.com/article/245628
4. Future of Learning, 'Helping students develop an entrepreneurial mindset', John Spenser, September 8, 2016, http://www.spencerauthor.com/helping-students-develop-an-entrepreneurial-mindset/.
5. The Lonely Entrepreneur, 'Types of entrepreneurs: Understanding the unique differences', August 13, 2018, https://lonelyentrepreneur.com/types-of-entrepreneurs/
6. Start your business, Important personal characteristics of entrepreneurs, Hiscox blogs, https://www.hiscox.com/blog/10-important-personal-characteristics-entrepreneurs
7. Getting down to business, Entrepreneurial profile, Éducation Loisir et sport, 2007, http://entrepreneuriat.inforoutefpt.org/documents/File/ANG_Profil.pdf

8. The balance small business, Seven stages of starting and running a business, Darrell Zahorsky, October 2019 https://www.thebalancesmb.com/find-your-business-life-cycle-2951237
9. Three ways to make your small business blossom, Jenna Cyprus, January 2016, http://www.smbceo.com/2016/01/06/3-ways-to-make-your-small-business-blossom/

Chapter 3

1. Guide, 'How to cultivate self-leadership to master your behavior and realize your leadership potential', Scott Jeffrey, https://scottjeffrey.com/self-leadership/
2. Why Self-Leadership Matters and How to Grow It, Mike Gingerich, https://www.mikegingerich.com/blog/why-self-leadership-matters-and-how-to-grow-it/
3. International Journal of Business and Social Science, 'Self-leadership: Why It Matters', Dr. Michelle Browning, February 2018, https://ijbssnet.com/journals/Vol_9_No_2_February_2018/2.pdf
4. Self-leadership Definition, Andrew Brayant, https://www.selfleadership.com/what-is-self-leadership
5. Thrive Global, 'The 4 Pillars of Self-Leadership: Time to Focus on You', Andrea Goodridge, September 2, 2019, https://thriveglobal.com/stories/the-4-pillars-of-self-leadership-time-to-focus-on-you/

Chapter 4

1. Innovation management, Improvement is not innovation, Patrick Lefler, August 24, 2010, https://innovationmanagement.se/imtool-articles/improvement-is-not-innovation/
2. Elevate, Knowing the difference between innovation and improvement, Ruth Henderson,

https://www.ellevatenetwork.com/articles/7022-knowing-the-difference-between-innovation-vs-improvement

3. Kainexus, Improvement or innovation, https://www.kainexus.com/continuous-improvement/innovation
4. How to add value to your products and service, Dragan Sutevski, https://www.entrepreneurshipinabox.com/13489/add-value-products-services/
5. The startup, 4 important benefits of innovation in business, Startup Hong Kong Limited, June 22, 2018, https://medium.com/swlh/4-important-benefits-of-innovation-in-business-64ed0d78d150
6. Use innovation to grow your business, Info Entrepreneurs, Canada Business Network, 2009, https://www.infoentrepreneurs.org/en/guides/use-innovation-to-grow-your-business/

Chapter 5

1. 9 Inexpensive Ways to Get Your Business Noticed Online, Jennifer Lonoff Schiff, 2014, https://www.cio.com/article/2475404/9-inexpensive-ways-to-get-your-new-business-noticed-online.html
2. 5 Tips for Attracting New Customers, Accino, https://us.accion.org/resource/5-tips-attracting-new-customers/
3. 7 Benefits of Branding Every Small Business Owner Should Know, Solid Creative, https://solidcreative.com/thoughts/7-benefits-of-branding-every-small-business-owner-should-know/
4. 11 Benefits of Branding Your Small Business, Lisa Cron Design, https://lisacron.design/blog/2017/8/11/11-benefits-of-branding-your-small-business
5. Eighteen Ways to Find Customers, Janet Attard, Business Know-How, updated in 2020,

https://www.businessknowhow.com/startup/findcustomers.htm

Chapter 6

1. 12 Small Business Bookkeeping Tips, Beginner Bookkeeping, https://www.beginner-bookkeeping.com/small-business-bookkeeping-tips.html
2. Basic Bookkeeping for Small Business, Informi Talking Small Business, https://www.beginner-bookkeeping.com/small-business-bookkeeping-tips.html
3. Why Business Reporting Is Important For Business Success, Melanie, Unleashed, https://www.unleashedsoftware.com/blog/why-business-reporting-is-important-for-business-success

Printed by Libri Plureos GmbH in Hamburg, Germany